SPIRIT OF FORGIVENESS

SESSION 10

DR. AARON R. JONES
Foreword by Dr. Timothy M. Hill

Interfacing Evangelism and Discipleship

WORKBOOK

Spirit of Forgiveness

Dr. Aaron R. Jones

Interfacing Evangelism and Discipleship – Spirit of Forgiveness

Copyright © 2018 by Dr. Aaron R. Jones

Printed in the United States of America

Published by Kingdom Publishing, LLC, Odenton, MD 21113

All rights reserved. No part of this book may be reproduced or transmitted in any form or by any means, electronic or mechanical, including photocopying, recording or by any information storage and retrieval system without written permission from the author, except for the inclusion of brief quotations in a review.

All scripture quotations are from the King James Version of the Bible. Thomas Nelson Publishers, Nashville: Thomas Nelson, Inc. 1972

Editor: Sharon D. Jones

Graphic Designer: Janell McIlwain – JM Virtual Concepts

                Tiara Smith

ISBN 978-1-947741-27-0

Table of Contents

Interfacing Evangelism and Discipleship Sessions 1

Foreword 2

FORGIVENESS

God's Power of Forgiveness 4

The Importance of Forgiveness 7

Scriptural Support for Forgiveness 11

A.C.T.

Admit 16

Confession 19

Transformation 22

About the Author

Contact Page

Interfacing Evangelism and Discipleship
Sessions

Session 1—**Introduction and Philosophy**

Session 2—**5 Principles to Encourage Evangelism**

Session 3—**Components of Evangelism**

Session 4—**Bait for Evangelism**

Session 5—**Methodology of Evangelism**

Session 6—**Church Planting Produces Evangelism and Discipleship**

Session 7—**Babes in Christ**

Session 8—**Components of Discipleship**

Session 9—**Evangelism and Discipleship Plan**

Session 10—**Spirit of Forgiveness**

Foreword

When God calls a man of faith and fortitude to a specific purpose in the building of His Kingdom, He uses an individual like Dr. Aaron Jones.

Feeling the urgency of the hour, Dr. Jones has shaped his participation in the FINISH Commitment by emphasizing the merging of evangelism and discipleship strategies to assist churches and individuals in their quests to effectively reach the lost. As Senior Pastor of New Hope Church of God, he is well-aware of what it takes to affect the Great Commission of our Lord.

Dr. Jones' desire is to instruct others on how to deliberately make an impact on winning souls and then discipling them for powerful Christian service. His all-inclusive approach will intrigue and provide the impetus for those willing to pursue the heart of God.

Interfacing Evangelism and Discipleship will change the course of your outreach!

Dr. Timothy M. Hill
General Overseer
Church of God, Cleveland, Tennessee

Forgiveness

> Our forgiveness should be the drive to fulfill our call to Evangelism and Discipleship.

God's Power of Forgiveness

God's Power of Forgiveness

- Doesn't Remember (Isaiah 43:25)

_____

_____

_____

_____

God's Power of Forgiveness

- East to West disposal (Psalm 103:12)

_____

_____

_____

_____

_____

- Sea Bound (Micah 7:20)

_____

_____

_____

_____

_____

Additional Notes

The Importance of Forgiveness

The Importance of Forgiveness

- The reason why we are able to forgive is because we were forgiven of all our sins.

___
___
___
___

Interfacing Evangelism and Discipleship – Spirit of Forgiveness

■ Evangelism and discipleship becomes easier when we have the heart of forgiveness.

_____
_____
_____
_____

■ Our approach to people must be in the spirit of forgiveness.

_____
_____
_____
_____

■ Lack of forgiveness interferes with our relationship with God.

_____
_____
_____
_____

The Importance of Forgiveness

■ Matthew 6:15— "But if ye forgive not men their trespasses, neither will your Father forgive your trespasses."

_____

_____

_____

_____

Additional Notes

Scriptural Support for Forgiveness

<u>Scriptural Support for Forgiveness</u>

■   "For if ye forgive men their trespasses, your heavenly Father will also forgive you." (Matthew 6:14)

_____

_____

_____

- "And be ye kind one to another, tenderhearted, forgiving one another, even as God for Christ's sake hath forgiven you." (Ephesians 4:32)

_____

_____

_____

_____

- "Then came Peter to him, and said, Lord, how oft shall my brother sin against me, and I forgive him? till seven times? Jesus saith unto him, I say not unto thee, Until seven times: but, Until seventy times seven." (Matthew 18:21, 22)

_____

_____

_____

_____

- "Forbearing one another, and forgiving one another, if any man have a quarrel against any: even as Christ forgave you, so also do ye." (Colossians 3:13)

_____

_____

_____

_____

Scriptural Support for Forgiveness

Additional Notes

A.C.T.

A.C.T.

(Taken from Dr. Philip Bonaparte and Dr. Wayne Solomon)

"He that covereth his sins shall not prosper: but whoso confesseth and forsaketh them shall have mercy."
Proverbs 28:13

Forgiveness is an A.C.T.[1]

- Admission
- Confession
- Transformation

Admit

Admission

"He that covereth his sins shall not prosper..."

- Refuse to cover the sin of unforgiveness any longer

_____
_____
_____

- Without admission we will continue to fall in unforgiveness.

_____
_____
_____

Admit

- Forgiveness cannot take place without God

_____

_____

_____

- We must admit and realize there is a problem.

_____

_____

_____

Additional Notes

Confession

Confession

"...but whoso confesseth..."

- Confession is the path to forgiveness. (1 John 1:9)

_____
_____
_____

- Confession is the path to being cleansed. (1 John 1:9)

_____
_____
_____

■ Confession is the path to righteousness. (1 John 1:9)

■ Confession is the path to healing. (James 5:16)

Confession

Additional Notes

Transformation

Transformation

"...forsaketh them shall have mercy."

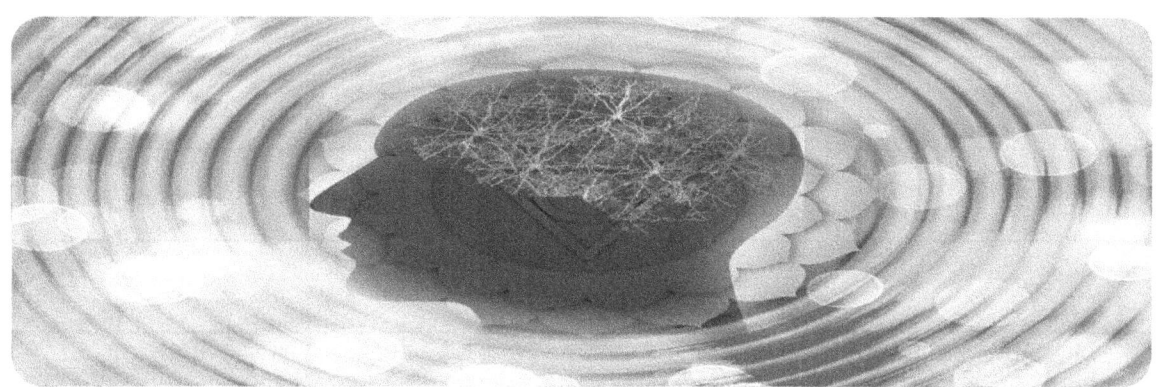

- I must change!

___

___

___

- "forsake"—abandon and be transformed

___

___

___

Transformation

- Romans 12:2—renewing the mind

_____

_____

_____

- Transformation takes place when there is a change of heart by the power of God.

_____

_____

_____

Additional Notes

About the Author

DR. AARON R. JONES serves as Senior Pastor of New Hope Church of God. Under his pastorate is New Hope Kiddie Kollege, Inc (Daycare) and New Hope Community Outreach Services, Inc. Dr. Jones also oversees New Hope Church of God Ghana (2 churches) and New Hope Church of God Uganda (3 churches).

Dr. Jones is an Ordained Bishop with the Church of God denomination and is the DELMARVA-DC District Overseer (16 churches). Dr. Jones serves on DELMARVA-DC's Regional Council, Ministerial Internship Program Board, Urban Ministry Committee, Finance Committee, and Chaplain's Board. He also serves on both the Church of God's International and DELMARVA-DC Ministry to the Military Board. In his local community, Dr. Jones serves as a Chaplain for the Charles County Sheriff Department. He also serves as Board Secretary for the United Ministers Coalition of Southern Maryland, Inc.

Being obedient to 2 Timothy 2:15, "Study to show thyself approved…," Dr. Jones received a Doctorate in Theology and Pastoral Counseling from Life

Christian University and a Doctorate in Christian Counseling from American Christian College and Seminary. He is a certified Pastoral Counselor with the International Association of Christian Counseling Professionals. He is a Life and Pastoral Coach. He is the former Executive Vice President of the National Bible College and Seminary in Fort Washington, Maryland.

Dr. Jones has published ten books and a soul-wining project that provide a biblical foundation for Christian doctrine and discipline. He has recorded a CD entitled, Peace in the Storm. He is the founder and owner of God's Comfort Ministries, LLC, which provides Christian literature, evangelism training, and spiritual guidance. He has appeared live on TCT Network; WATC-TV's Atlanta Live; Babbie's House (hosted by CCM artist Babbie Mason); and In Concert Today on DCTV. He has done radio interviews with Radio One's WYCB's program; The Praise Fest Show; and online with Total Prayze. He was featured on the cover of Change Gospel Magazine and interviewed on Promoting Purpose Magazine.

Dr. Jones not only serves God, but his country as well. He has served over 20 years in the Armed Forces. He is a retired Chaplain with the Army National Guard. He participated in both Operation Noble Eagle (2003) and Operation Iraqi Freedom III (2005).

Dr. Jones is happily married to the former Sharon Russell. He sincerely believes without her love, support, and encouragement, many of his goals would not have been accomplished.

Contact Page

Mailing Address:

150 Post Office Road #1079

Waldorf, Maryland 20604

Website: www.godscomfort.net

Email: drjones@godscomfortmin.net

Facebook: God's Comfort Ministries

Twitter: @GodsComfort_Min

Instagram: @godscomfort_min

GOD'S COMFORT MINISTRIES

God's Comfort Ministries (GCM) provides practical Christian books, teachings, trainings, and coaching to new converts and seasoned believers. GCM provides understanding of the doctrinal principles of the Bible.

Services Provided

Pastoral and Life Coaching

Evangelism and Discipleship Training

Spiritual Guidance

New Author Consultation

Christian Literature

www.ingramcontent.com/pod-product-compliance
Lightning Source LLC
Chambersburg PA
CBHW081358080526
44588CB00016B/2532

www.ingramcontent.com/pod-product-compliance
Lightning Source LLC
Chambersburg PA
CBHW081358080526
44588CB00016B/2532